AF131442

BOOK ANALYSIS

Written by Laura Clements

The Moonstone

BY WILKIE COLLINS

WILKIE COLLINS

AN ENGLISH NOVELIST OF THE VICTORIAN ERA

- **Born in London in 1824.**
- **Died in London in 1889.**
- **Notable works:**
  - *The Woman in White* (1859), novel
  - *No Name* (1862), novel
  - *Armadale* (1866), novel

Wilkie Collins was born in London, where he spent most of his adult life. He was baptised as 'William Wilkie Collins' but chose to drop the 'William' in adulthood, which the *Oxford Dictionary of National Biography* describes as being "typical of his dislike of formality". It was when Collins was sent to boarding school that he discovered his talents as a story-teller, which he allegedly used to appease his childhood bullies. After completing his education, his first job was as a clerk in the Strand office of a tea merchant, yet he was disengaged with his job and spent his office hours writing. Even after leaving his work to pursue a career in writing, Collins remained intrigued with the legal world, which is reflected in his novels. Collins met fellow writer Charles Dickens (1812-1870) in 1851, leading to one of the most lucrative friendships of his life, as he became a regular contributor to Dickens' periodicals. Collins suffered with poor health throughout his adult life and died of bronchitis in his home. The popularity of Collins' work declined after his death, with the exception of his two most celebrated novels: *The Woman in White* and *The Moonstone.*

THE MOONSTONE

A CLASSIC ENGLISH DETECTIVE NOVEL

- **Genre:** novel
- **Reference edition:** Collins, W. (1999) *The Moonstone*. Oxford: Oxford University Press.
- **1ˢᵗ edition:** 1868
- **Themes:** imperialism, theft, trade, imported goods, diamonds, mystery, medical advancements

The Moonstone was published in magazine instalments during the Victorian era, and is considered to be the founding novel of the English detective genre. The plot follows the fate of the titular Moonstone from its origins in India, to its theft by an English military man who places it in the hands of his family. The novel is concerned with its disappearance from an English country home in the late 1840s. Collins' writing is meticulously detailed, and sweeps the reader off on a quest to unwrap the mystery. The novel is narrated by a series of characters, all of whom harbour their own knowledge about the Moonstone's disappearance. Therefore, it is the role of the reader to piece together the different strands of this narrative and find the notorious Moonstone. Subsequent detective works, both literary and on-screen, owe themselves to this pivotal tale by Collins.

SUMMARY

THE BIRTHDAY PARTY

At her 18th birthday party, Miss Rachel is gifted the Moonstone diamond, which was stolen from a Hindu tribe by her late uncle, who was a member of the English army. She wears the Diamond around her neck during her party and puts it safely in her sitting-room cabinet before bed. When Rachel wakes up in the morning, the diamond has been taken from her cabinet and an investigation ensues. The Indian jugglers who entertained at Rachel's birthday closely watch the family, and it is suspected by several characters that they are connected to the Hindus who are trying to retrieve their Diamond. Lady Verinder, the lady of the house, disapproves of the gift that has been brought into the family home by her daughter's suitor Franklin Blake. Sergeant Cuff is assigned to the case, and starts directing accusations at members of the household, such as the maid Rosanna Spearman, and even at Miss Rachel herself.

THE SHIVERING SAND

Suspicion lingers around Rosanna Spearman, and it is revealed that she has committed suicide. Franklin Blake follows the trail to find out more about her suspected involvement in the theft. It becomes clear that Rosanna Spearman went to excessive lengths to conceal a package before taking her life. Having followed the directions in a letter he received from Rosanna, Franklin Blake was told to "do what you are told to do in the memorandum enclosed with this – and do it without any person being present to overlook you" (p. 302). These instructions lead him down the beach, where he pulls a tin out of the quicksand. The tin contains a nightgown with a red paint stain (from Rachel's freshly painted door on the night of the theft), with his own name on the label. It is revealed that Rosanna found a paint stain on Franklin's bedclothes which she had tried to hide in order to protect him, as she was in love with him. Previously, the wet door had been mentioned in the early stages of the investigation when a smear was noticed in the fresh paintwork, but Sergeant Cuff dismissed Superintendent Seegrave's belief that it could be evidence, since the paint would have been *"eight hours dry"* by the time any of the servants were tending to the room. This clue, left by Rosanna, is the most pivotal point in revealing who took the Moonstone from Rachel's cabinet. Rosanna committed suicide because she could not manage to get Franklin's attention to warn him of his involvement, despite her efforts to protect him.

DR. CANDY'S OPIUM

After this revelation, Franklin Blake meets with Rachel. She tells him outright that she saw him take the Moonstone from her cabinet, but decided to keep it a secret to protect both of their reputations. This explains why Rachel acted disinterested towards the investigation procee-dings, and why she shunned Franklin when she had previously been affectionate towards him. Having had this conversation with Rachel, Franklin returns to Yorkshire where he meets Ezra Jennings, the assistant to Dr. Candy who fell ill on the night of the birthday celebrations a year earlier. Jennings recounts how, on the night of Rachel's dinner party, the doctor "found an urgent message from a patient, waiting for him; and he most unfortunately went at once to visit the sick person, without stopping to change his clothes" (p. 367) which caused him to come down with a fever the next day. This sickness left Dr. Candy incapacitated throughout the investigation. Franklin Blake reveals to Jennings that a year ago he had been sleeping badly, but the night of the party was an exception. Jennings asks Blake if he remembers "having entered into anything like a dispute with [Dr. Candy] – at the birthday dinner, or afterwards – on the subject of his profession?" (p. 380). This question prompts Blake to remember that he had "attacked the art of medicine at the dinner-table with sufficient rashness and sufficient pertinacity to put even Mr Candy out of temper for a moment" (*ibid.*). Jennings then reveals that Dr. Candy secretly gave Blake opium without his knowing because of the criticisms that he made, which caused him to take the Diamond in a trance. His taking of the Moonstone was provoked by his worries for its safety in the house. This is affirmed when they re-enact the events of the evening. This demonstrates how Franklin Blake was used as a medical experiment, which reflects the developing scientific knowledge of the Victorian era in England.

ABLEWHITE THE SAILOR

At the close of the novel, the Moonstone is traced to a waterside inn which contains the body of a dead man but no diamond. The corpse's true identity is revealed when they notice that the sailor is wearing a disguise and Sergeant Cuff "traced with his finger a thin line of livid white, running backward from the dead man's forehead, between the swarthy complexion, and the slightly-disturbed black hair" (p. 444). Having pulled the corpse's well-hidden disguise away, it becomes clear that the body is none other than Ablewhite, Rachel's cousin and ex-fiancé. Blake and Cuff find out that Ablewhite was about to travel to Amsterdam and have the stone cut up to replenish a trust fund that he had embezzled from, and that he has used the Moonstone as a surety for a loan. As such, he took advantage of Franklin's opium-induced state by taking the Diamond for himself, as opposed to returning it to the bank as he was asked. However, Ablewhite was killed by the Indian jugglers before he managed to board his ship to Amsterdam. When the mystery is solved, Rachel and Franklin are reconciled and married.

The epilogue by the adventurer Mr. Murthwaite reveals how the Moonstone was returned to India and placed in the forehead of the statue of the Moon God, where it was originally found by Colonel Herncastle in the novel's prologue.

CHARACTER STUDY

GABRIEL BETTEREDGE

The household steward of Lady Verinder, for whom he has worked for his entire life. He is asked by the family to write a record of the case of the stolen Moonstone, which amounts to the first period of the story.

MISS RACHEL

Miss Rachel is given the diamond by her uncle as a gift for her 18th birthday. She places the diamond in her Indian cabinet overnight and it is stolen. Betteredge believes that the diamond is acting like a kind of curse upon Rachel, stating that "someone is bound to put this plaguey Diamond into Miss Rachel's hands on her birthday" (p. 43). Rachel rejects Ablewhite's offer of marriage because she is in love with Franklin, but loses trust in him after she sees him take the Moonstone. However, she does eventually agree to marry Godfrey, but breaks off the engagement when she comes to believe that he is marrying her for the money she has inherited through her mother's death. Rachel becomes reluctant to open up after the theft of the Moonstone, yet seems distraught at the accusations that she may have been involved in its disappearance. She is a very loyal character, and will stop at nothing to protect Franklin Blake despite her distrust in him.

EZRA JENNINGS

Ezra Jennings is Dr. Candy's medical assistant, who helps Franklin Blake to discover how he took the Moonstone. The *Oxford Dictionary of National Biography* (ODNB) recounts how Collins was very ill whilst writing *The Moonstone*, and that Jennings' use of laudanum to manage his symptoms is a reflection of Collins' own experiences with illness.

MR FRANKLIN BLAKE

Mr Franklin Blake sits at the centre of the novel's romance plot though his love for Miss Rachel. He is appointed to give the Diamond to Rachel on her 18th birthday, and he is also the character who takes it from the cabinet under the influence of opium. It is his trusting nature that causes the

Moonstone's disappearance when he hands it to Godfrey Ablewhite to return it to the bank. He has no memory of taking the Moonstone, but a conversation with Rachel reveals that she saw him make off with it with her own eyes. However, Franklin's belief in his own innocence drives the rest of the plot as he attempts to clear himself of blame. Mr Franklin is more of a detective than Sergeant Cuff, and of all the characters in the novel, he is the one who will stop at nothing to find the Moonstone to prove himself to Miss Rachel.

DR. CANDY

Dr. Candy fell ill on the night of Rachel's birthday and does not recover until the investigation has come to an end. His assistant, Ezra Jennings, reveals that the doctor gave Franklin a dose of Opium without his knowledge on the night of the theft to settle a dispute over modern medicine.

JOHN HERNCASTLE

Herncastle is introduced in the prologue; he fought in the British army against India, and stole the Moonstone from them in 1799. He is Rachel's uncle and leaves the Diamond to her as an inheritance. As the plot unravels, it becomes evident that this gift was given in an attempt to bring ill fortune upon Lady Verinder's family.

MR GODFREY ABLEWHITE

Godfrey Ablewhite is a well-known philanthropist of exceedingly good reputation: "He loved everybody. And everybody loved *him*" (p. 55). Despite his trickery and direct involvement with the Moonstone's disappearance, he is initially described favourably as "a good Samaritan by choice" who was involved with "Maternal societies for confining poor women; Magdelen societies for rescuing poor women" (p. 54). Ablewhite's involvement with growing social change paints a portrait of him as a positive and caring person. Ablewhite successfully proposes marriage to Rachel; however, the engagement is cancelled after Rachel finds out he is trying to access the fortune she has inherited. Later, Franklin and Cuff trace the Diamond back to a sailor who has been killed. The dead sailor is then revealed to be Ablewhite, who has been living in disguise. When Godfrey is found, the news breaks that he had previously pawned the Moonstone, and having reclaimed it again was planning to take it to Amsterdam and have it cut up.

ROSANNA SPEARMAN

Rosanna Spearman is one of Lady Verinder's housemaids, a reformed thief, whom Sergeant Cuff believes to have been involved in the disappearance of the diamond because of her past. Rosanna is in love with Franklin Blake and, after concealing information that points to his involvement with the theft, she commits suicide. Sergeant Cuff believes that Rachel was using Rosanna to help her sell the Moonstone in order to pay off private debts.

SERGEANT CUFF

Sergeant Cuff is dismissed from the case for his belief that Rachel was involved in the theft of her own Diamond, in collusion with Rosanna Spearman. Cuff is the professional investigator of the narrative, who continues to attempt to solve the mystery even when he has been removed from his post.

ANALYSIS

BRITAIN AND INDIA

Collins' Moonstone is a fictional stone that echoes the Koh-i-Noor diamond of the Victorian era, which was taken from India and given to Queen Victoria after the British conquest of Punjab (1849). As such, the Moonstone is symbolic of tense national relations between Britain and India. Betteredge describes the diamond as being "as large, or nearly, as a plover's egg! The light that streamed from it was like the light of the harvest moon. When you looked down into the stone, you looked into a yellow deep that drew your eyes into it so that they saw nothing else" (p. 61). This description reflects the appearance of the Koh-i-Noor diamond which is now part of the British crown jewels. The prologue builds this contextual link as it recounts the Storming of Seringapatam, which took place under General Baird (British military leader, 1757-1829) on 4 May 1799, in an extract from a family paper. The paper recounts how John Herncastle took the diamond during the siege, and how the narrator believes that "he will live to regret it, if he keeps the Diamond; and that others will live to regret taking it from him, if he gives the Diamond away" (p. 6). Melissa Free argues that "though Collins' contemporaries were familiar with 'empire', they tended to perceive it as something that existed outside of, but not as part of, nation, and his nineteenth-century reviewers – no doubt as a consequence of this belief – did not see *The Moonstone* as a piece of social criticism" (2006: 344).

As such, the diamond is frequently associated with colonialist language. After a conversation with Mr Franklin about their "quiet English house suddenly invaded by a devilish Indian diamond" (p. 33) he contrasts this oriental superstition against growing colonialism in England. Betteredge asks, "who ever heard the like of it – in the nineteenth century, mind; in an age of progress, and in a country which rejoices in the blessings of the British constitution?" (*ibid.*). In addition, Robert McCrum argues that the prologue "connects every detail of the plot to the great imperial drama of India, the society over which Queen Victoria would eventually declare herself 'Empress'. From the outset, the

Indian factor imbues the tale with the sinister mystery of the East" (2014). The eventual fate of the diamond is revealed at the end of the novel in a letter written from Mr Murthwaite to Mr Bruff (dated 1850). Murthwaite writes that he has travelled from the region of Kattiawar to the city of Somnauth to witness a ceremony in honour of the god of the Moon. He recounts how:

> "There, raised high on a throne, seated on his typical antelope, with his four arms stretching towards the four corners of the earth – there, soared above us, dark and awful in the mystic light of heaven, the god of the Moon. And there, in the forehead of the deity, gleamed the yellow Diamond, whose splendour had last shone on me in England, from the bosom of a woman's dress!" (p. 466)

As such, the Moonstone represents India rebelling against English colonial rule.

RACIAL TENSIONS

These ideas of colonial tensions also translate into matters of race. Betteridge narrates that "the Devil (or the Diamond) possessed that dinner party" (p. 69). The gives the idea that the

Moonstone, which originates from the Hindus, establishes an atmosphere of racial tension as a source of exotic 'evil' in the narrative. There are many other malevolent illustrations of race in the narrative, such as the "false brown face" (p. 304) of the quicksand that hides Blake's nightgown, the faces of the Indians who permeate the narrative, and the painted face of the disguised Godfrey Ablewhite. These images associate orientalism with mystery and concealment in the novel. The Moonstone itself is also related to images of darkness; when Rachel receives the Moonstone, Betteridge records that Lady Verinder "took the blackest view possible of the Colonel's motives, and that she was bent on getting the Moonstone out of her daughter's possession at the first opportunity" (p. 62). However, it is unfair to call *The Moonstone* a 'racist' novel, since it has to be examined within its own context. In Victorian England, the eastern world was viewed as mysterious and unknown, a barbarian civilisation to be civilised by English colonialism. As such, this imported Diamond and everything that touches it is expressed by Collins as having been contaminated by a foreign influence.

THE MODERN CRIME NOVEL

The Moonstone is often referred to as the first detective novel; however, the ODNB contests this claim, stating that, "although not the first detective story, it is a classic of the genre, with many features repeatedly borrowed by later writers such as Arthur Conan Doyle, Agatha Christie, and Dorothy Sayers". The novel is divided into two periods; the first period describes the disappearance of the Moonstone, as narrated by Gabriel Betteredge, and then the second period contains eight different narratives. As such, the novel creates an effect of patchwork evidence that comes together in the final revelation. The readers of the novel become Collins' detectives. Melissa Free argues that "to underscore – to solicit, even – the reader's active interpretive role, Collins structures the text as an archival document, constructs the plot as a mystery, and positions fictional and actual readers as both judges and detectives" (p. 341). Free's argument demonstrates how the archival layout of Collins' novel puts the reader in a position where they are literally piecing together the parts of the mystery. Free continues, "the compilation of letters, reports, notes, newspaper clippings, journal entries, wills, and even a receipt [...] serves as testimony for the reader's consideration" (*ibid.*).

SENSATIONALISM

The Victorian print press grew with the introduction of publishing in newspapers, and *The Moonstone* was, as John Sutherland puts it in his introductory notes to the novel, "first published in a twopenny newspaper format, in bulletin-length instalments" (1999: xxiv). As such, *The Moonstone* was originally serialised in Dickens' magazine *All The Year Round* (January-August 1868). Serial publications made novels more affordable for middle class readers who might have struggled to pay for a novel upfront. Sensation fiction was published in newspapers, and the ODNB states that Collins came to be seen as the originator of the 'sensation novel', a term that was used by reviewers to describe his four best-known novels that were written in the 1860s. These novels included *The Woman in White, No Name* (1862), *Armadale* (1866), and *The Moonstone.* Mary Elizabeth Leighton and Lisa Surridge discuss how Collins also had *The*

Moonstone published in *Harper's Weekly*, an American literary magazine. They argue that the text is a lot like the notorious diamond, as "Collins's own text circulated as a commodity in the publishing market" of England and America (2009: 209), in the same way that the Moonstone circulated in various forms, such as being a piece of jewellery as well as an eastern religious symbol. Leighton and Surridge also highlight how *Harper's Weekly* transformed *The Moonstone* by including images. They state that, "the illustrators for *Harper's Weekly* chose to heighten the sensational atmosphere of Collins's text by means of interative scenes of darkness and turbulence, scenes of borders and boundary crossings" (p. 218).

THE EAST INDIA COMPANY

The East India Company was a trading alliance between England and India which facilitated the trading of everyday goods as well as narcotics and new medicines. The opium trade was growing rapidly in the Victorian era, which explains its role in the novel. Sutherland argues that "the opium trade was justified (in the colonial mind) by the insatiable British demand for tea and silks, and Chinese obstinacy in declining any reciprocal exports from the British Empire. The only way the trade could be balanced was by forcing a product on the Chinese" (p. xxi). Sutherland also elaborates that opium is the second most important subject of the narrative, because:

> "[T]he diamond is bequeathed to his niece by an opium smoker. It is subsequently stolen under the influence of opium. The solution to the crime is staged through the experimental application of opium by an opium addict. And, to cap it all off, the novel itself was written by another opium eater, so drugged – as he later claimed – that he could not even remember writing large parts of the novel." (p. xx)

Therefore, the trading relationship between Britain and India motivated the plot as heavily as it did the writer.

FURTHER REFLECTION

SOME QUESTIONS TO THINK ABOUT...

- How far does *The Moonstone* exhibit modernising forms of communication?
- To what extent should Franklin Blake be blamed for Rosanna Spearman's death?
- Do you think it is significant that the vast majority of the plot is set in Yorkshire as opposed to London?
- Could we consider Miss Rachel to be an accomplice in the theft for protecting Franklin Blake, and what do you think her motivations for this were?
- Who is the more effective investigator, Sergeant Cuff or Franklin Blake?
- Compare the different narrators featured in the novel. Are some of them more reliable than others?
- What methods of surveillance are used in the narrative?

- How much does Franklin Blake's somnambulism reveal about the growth of medical knowledge in Victorian England?
- How many 'new' Victorian ideas does Collins include in the narrative?

We want to hear from you!
Leave a comment on your online library
and share your favourite books on social media!

FURTHER READING

REFERENCE EDITION

- Collins, W. (1999) *The Moonstone*. Oxford: Oxford University Press.

REFERENCE STUDIES

- Free, M. (2006) "Dirty Linen": Legacies of Empire in Wilkie Collins's *The Moonstone. Texas Studies in Literature and Language*, 48(4).

- Leighton, M. E., and Surridge, L. (2009) The Transatlantic Moonstone: A Study of the Illustrated Serial in Harper's Weekly. *Victorian Periodicals Review*, 42(3), pp. 207-243.

- McCrum, R. (2014) An introduction to *The Moonstone. British Library*. [Online]. [Accessed 5 December 2018]. Available from: <https://www.bl.uk/romantics-and-victorians/articles/an-introduction-to-the-moonstone>

- Peters, C. (2011) Collins, (William) Wilkie. *The Oxford Dictionary of National Biography*. [Online]. [Accessed 30 November 2018]. Available from: <https://doi.org/10.1093/ref:odnb/5961>

- Sutherland, J. (1999) Introductory material to *The Moonstone* by Wilkie Collins. Oxford: Oxford University Press, pp. vii-xlix.

ADAPTATIONS

- *The Moonstone.* (2016) [Television series]. Lisa Mulcahy. Dir. UK: BBC.

MORE FROM BRIGHTSUMMARIES.COM

- Reading guide – *The Woman in White* by Wilkie Collins.

www.brightsummaries.com

Ebook EAN: 9782808016131

Paperback EAN: 9782808016148

Legal Deposit: D/2018/12603/567

Cover: © Primento

Digital conception by Primento, the digital partner of
publishers.